Czech Style Recip

Your Cookbook for Bohemian Breakfasts, Dinners Desserts

BY: Allie Allen

COOK & ENJOY

Copyright 2020 Allie Allen

Copyright Notes

Table of Contents

Introduction

Why do Czech recipes seem to be interesting to make?

Can you make authentic dishes right in your own home?

Will it be difficult to find the ingredients you'll need?

Czech cooking often uses fat for flavor, grease to heat, and cholesterol-laden ingredients. While most food markets in the Western world tend to offer healthier foods, you can still find the ingredients you'll use to make recipes that are true to their Czech heritage.

Dining in the Czech Republic reflects many influences from countries that are neighbors in Europe. From Germany came dumplings and sauerkraut. Vienna offers schnitzels,

Hungary has goulash. Other Slavic countries bring pickles, sour vegetables, vinegar, and sour cream to the table – literally.

You'll enjoy the meats that dominate Czech dinners. Roast pork is quite popular and is often served with dumplings and sauerkraut. Other, less formal meals are quick and filling and are usually accompanied by side dishes of dumplings.

Don't forget the drinks! Czech beer is among the best in the world. There are many brands, and they're almost all great. Enjoy the new world of old-world cooking.

Czech breakfasts can be sweet or savory, but they're all tasty, no doubt about it. Try one of these favorites...

1 – Czech Palačinky

Palačinky are pancakes with the consistency of crepes, rolled tightly with sweet strawberry jam. You can serve them with fresh berries or whipped cream.

Makes 4 Servings

Cooking + Prep Time: 25 minutes

Ingredients:

For the batter

- 2 cups milk, 2%
- 2 eggs, large
- 1 tbsp. of sugar, granulated
- 1/4 tsp. of salt, kosher
- 1 cup of flour, all-purpose
- Oil, vegetable

For the filling

- Preserves or jams, fruit, your favorites
- Top with whipped cream, fresh fruit, cocoa powder, powdered sugar, ice cream, etc.

Instructions:

1. Mix the salt flour together.

2. Mix 2% milk, whisked eggs and sugar together.

3. Add wet ingredients slowly into flour mixture and combine till you have a smooth texture.

4. Grease non-stick pan lightly. Allow oil to get hot. Pour thin batter layer into pan.

5. When one side has cooked, about two minutes, flip crepe. After second side cooks, slide from pan to plate.

6. Spread jam or preserves all over crepe and roll it up. Add desired toppings. Serve promptly.

2 – Kolache

These tasty treats are staples in farm kitchens and bakeries in the Czech Republic. Their flavor is best enjoyed warm from your oven.

Makes 24 Servings

Cooking + Prep Time: 1 hour 5 minutes + 2 hours 15 minutes rising time

Ingredients:

- 1/2 cup of water, warm
- 2 x 1/4-oz. pkg's. of dry yeast, active
- 1 cup of milk, warm
- 1/2 cup of sugar, granulated
- 1 tsp. of salt, kosher
- 1/2 cup of shortening, melted
- 2 cups of sifted flour, all-purpose
- 2 eggs, large
- 3 1/2 more cups + 2 tbsp. of flour, all-purpose
- 2 yolks from large eggs
- 3 tbsp. of sugar, granulated
- 1/8 tsp. of salt, kosher
- 1 cup of raisins, golden
- 2 cups of cottage cheese, small curd

Instructions:

1. Pour the yeast in 1/2 cup lukewarm water and set it aside for soaking.

2. In separate bowl, combine 1 cup of milk, 1/2 cup of sugar and 1 tsp. of kosher salt. Add 2 cups of sifted flour and 1/2 cup of melted shortening. Add two beaten eggs and the yeast mixture. Combine well and set aside till spongy and bubbly.

3. Add 3 1/2 cups flour to mixture. Blend it well. Set the bowl aside for an hour to rise. Punch the dough down and set aside for another hour to rise again.

4. Beat together 2 yolks, 3 tbsp. of sugar, 2 tbsp. of flour, 1/8 tsp. of kosher salt and the cup of golden raisins. Add the cottage cheese. Combine well.

5. Pinch 1" balls off dough. Press indentations in middle of them. Add filling into indentations. Allow to rise for 12-15 minutes.

6. Bake in 425F oven for 13-18 minutes, till golden. Serve.

3 – Livance Pancakes

Who doesn't love pancakes? They can be made in so many ways, with fruits and nuts, and made fluffy or thin.

Makes 6 Servings

Cooking + Prep Time: 50 minutes + 1 hour rising time

Ingredients:

- 1 cup of milk, 2%
- 2 tbsp. of butter, unsalted
- 1 1/2 cups of flour, all-purpose
- 1 tsp. of yeast, dry, active
- 1 1/2 tsp. of salt, kosher
- 1 tbsp. of sugar, granulated
- 1 egg, medium
- To cook: butter or oil

Instructions:

1. Warm milk butter together in small-sized pan till butter starts melting.

2. Whisk dry ingredients together in med-sized bowl. Pour milk mixture in with dry ingredients. Combine well. Beat in egg.

3. Cover bowl with cling wrap. Allow to rise for an hour or so. It should be quite liquid and very bubbly.

4. Heat large-sized skillet on med-low. Coat skillet with butter. It is ready to cook when butter is gently sizzling.

5. Use ladle to drop 1/4 cup batter in pan. Form two or three pancakes in pan to cook, without crowding them.

6. Cook pancakes for three minutes or so and turn when surface forms bubbles. First side should be golden brown in color. Cook for three minutes more. Top with syrup or jam and serve.

There are so many traditional Czech recipes for lunches, dinners, appetizers and snacks. Here are some of the best...

4 – Beef Goulash

Following this recipe will yield delicious, classic goulash. The meat will fall apart just with a fork, and the caramelized onions add to the taste.

Makes 3-4 Servings

Cooking + Prep Time: 2 1/4 hours

Ingredients:

- 1 1/2 pounds of cubed beef
- 2 tbsp. of oil, vegetable
- 1 diced onion, large
- 1/2 chopped pepper, green
- 2 tbsp. of paprika +/- as desired
- 1 1/2 tsp. of salt, kosher
- 1/2 cup of water, filtered

Instructions:

1. Heat the oil in skillet. Add the onion. Cook on low till yellowed slightly.

2. Add paprika. Combine well. Then add water, meat, salt and green peppers.

3. Cover skillet. Simmer till meat becomes tender, 1 1/2 – 2 hours or so.

4. Serve with dumplings on top or over boiled potatoes.

5 – Czech Haluski

Traditionally, this dish is made with Czech goat cheese. Since you generally won't find that outside of Europe, you can use brick or feta cheese. The taste will still wow you.

Makes 8 Servings

Cooking + Prep Time: 1 hour 5 minutes

Ingredients:

- 1 lb. of bacon, lean
- 4 peeled, chopped potatoes, small
- 1 cup of flour, all-purpose
- 2 beaten eggs, large
- 1/2 tsp. of baking powder
- 2 cups of Wisconsin cheese shreds
- A pinch of salt, kosher

Instructions:

1. Cook the bacon in large-sized skillet on med-high. Turn it occasionally, till browned evenly, 8-10 minutes or so. Drain bacon on plate lined with paper towels. When the bacon has cooled, crumble it. Set it aside.

2. Place the potatoes in food processor. Process till pureed well, two or three minutes. Transfer to bowl. Add and stir flour, salt and baking powder. Set the sticky dough aide.

3. Next, pour large-sized pot 1/2 filled with salted water. Bring to boil. Ladle spoonfuls of dough onto cutting board. Cut into pieces of about 1 tbsp. each. As pieces are cut, drop them into boiling water. Allow the dumplings to boil on med. heat till they float to top, usually a couple minutes. Remove the dumplings to large bowl.

4. Sprinkle the crumbled bacon and handful of cheese shreds over batches of dumplings. Continue to make them, then boil and transfer them to bowl. Sprinkle all with bacon crumbles and cheese shreds. After you have made all the dumplings, stir gently and combine all the ingredients. Serve.

6 – Carrot Stew

Although the name of this dish is carrot stew, it includes pork and bouillon, as well. It is often served with dinner rolls.

Makes 7 Servings

Cooking + Prep Time: 1 hour 25 minutes

Ingredients:

- 2 pounds of pork
- 2 tsp. of salt, kosher
- 6 cups of water, filtered
- 8 cups of carrots, diced
- 1 beef bouillon cube
- 1/2 onion, chopped

Instructions:

1. Add water, salt, pork and chopped onion to pressure cooker. Close lid. Bring to boil with high heat setting. Once the cooker begins hissing, reduce temperature to med-low. Cook for 35-40 minutes.

2. As meat cooks, peel cube eight cups of medium carrots.

3. To open pressure cooker, place in sink. Pour cold water over top of lid. Remove meat from water. Place on work surface and cut in smaller-sized cubes. Cover meat with cling wrap.

4. Add carrots to broth. Add 1 beef bouillon cube and 1/2 tsp. of salt. Cover. Bring back up to a boil.

5. Turn down heat. Cook for 12-15 minutes more. Open pressure cooker as you did above. Place pot back on stove with no lid. Add cut meat to carrots. Bring to boil.

6. In small pan, melt 6 tbsp. butter. Add 4 tbsp. flour. Mix flour into butter, stirring constantly. You'll note the rouge changing color. Remove frying pan from burner once color is dark pink.

7. Pour rouge into stew. Stir promptly. Cook for three to five minutes more. Serve stew with rolls.

7 – Roast Pork

Here is a very traditional meal from the Czech Republic, which is generally served on weekends. It goes well with dumplings and sauerkraut.

Makes 8 Servings

Cooking + Prep Time: 3 1/2 hours

Ingredients:

- 2 tbsp. of oil, vegetable
- 1 tbsp. of mustard, prepared
- 1 tbsp. of garlic powder
- 2 tbsp. of caraway seeds
- 1 tbsp. of salt, kosher
- 2 tsp. of pepper, ground
- 5 lbs. of blade roast, pork shoulder
- 3 chopped onions, medium
- 1/2 cup of beer
- 2 tbsp. of butter, unsalted
- 1 tbsp. of corn starch

Instructions:

1. Form paste in bowl with oil, seeds, mustard, salt, garlic powder and ground pepper. Rub this over the roast. Allow roast to sit for about 1/2 hour.

2. Preheat the oven to 350F.

3. Arrange onions in bottom of large-sized roast pan. Add beer. Place roast with the fat side facing down, on onions. Cover pan with aluminum foil.

4. Roast for one hour in 350F oven. Remove the foil. Turn the roast, scoring fat. Continue to roast for 2 1/2 hours, till internal temperature is at least 145F.

5. Remove roast from oven. Reserve the juices in pan. Allow roast to sit for 15-20 minutes, then slice it thinly.

6. Bring reserved juices from pan to boil in saucepan. Add corn starch and butter for thickening. Lower the heat. Simmer for five to 10 minutes or so. Serve along with pork.

8 – Bread Dumplings

These dumplings are quite typical side dishes served with main dishes of meat and gravy. They make three large or four medium dumplings that are sliced before serving.

Makes 4 Servings

Cooking + Prep Time: 45 minutes

Ingredients:

- 1 cup of lukewarm milk, 2%
- 1 tsp. of sugar, granulated
- 1 tbsp. of dry yeast, active
- 4 cups of flour, all-purpose
- 1/4 cup of warm water, filtered
- 2 tsp. of salt, kosher
- 2 eggs, large
- 4 cups of cubed bread, white

Instructions:

1. Warm the milk with sugar in small-sized bowl for 35-40 seconds in your microwave. It should be warm, yet not overly hot. Add the yeast. Stir milk in and set aside, allowing mixture to foam.

2. Add the water, flour, eggs, yeast mixture and kosher salt to mixing bowl. Mix with dough mixer for a few minutes. Add cubed bread and combine.

3. Remove dough to clean work surface. Use your hands to knead it. Divide into three or four pieces of the same size. Knead each individually. Then roll them into cylindrical shapes. Cover with cloth. Allow to rest for 8-10 minutes or so.

4. Pour water in 2 large-sized pots, with three inches or more in each. Bring to boil. Place a couple dumplings per pot. Stir so they won't stick.

5. Cover the pots with lids. Return to boil on med. Set lid a bit to the side so steam can escape. Boil for 8-10 minutes. Rotate the dumplings 180 degrees and continue to cook for 10 minutes more.

6. Make room on your work surface. Remove lids from pots. Slide spatula under middle of dumpling and remove it quickly from the water to your workspace. Poke it with fork, so steam escapes. This step should be done quickly.

7. To slice dumpling, first place thread under it. Wrap around top. Cross like you're going to tie a regular knot. Pull the thread tightly, which will cut slices of 1/2 inch each. Repeat steps with remainder of dumplings. Cover and serve warm.

9 – Cooked Cabbage

This is a perennial favorite dish in the Czech Republic. At dinner parties, you may find numerous versions of the dish, and the bowls will all be emptied.

Makes 10 Servings

Cooking + Prep Time: 35 minutes

Ingredients:

- 1 shredded head of cabbage, large
- 1/4 lb. of chopped bacon, lean
- 1 tbsp. of oil, vegetable
- 1 chopped onion, small
- 1 chopped celery stalk
- 1/4 cup of chopped bell pepper, green
- 3 tbsp. of vinegar, white
- 1/2 tsp. of salt, kosher
- 1 tsp. of pepper, ground

Instructions:

1. Bring large-sized pot of salted water to boil. Briefly blanche cabbage, then remove it and drain well.

2. In large-sized skillet, brown the bacon on med. heat till opaque. Then remove it and drain on a plate lined with paper towels.

3. Remove bacon grease, except for 1 tbsp. reserved, from skillet. Add 1 tbsp. oil. Heat on medium. Add bell pepper, onions and celery. Sauté till tender-crisp.

4. In large-sized bowl, combine cabbage, vegetable mixture with oil, bacon and vinegar. Season using kosher salt ground pepper. Combine well. Serve while warm.

10 – Tomato Salad

This tomato salad is an acidic dish, and quite refreshing. It is generally served as a side dish along with a filling main.

Makes 4 Servings

Cooking + Prep Time: 1/2 hour

Ingredients:

- 1 cup of water, filtered
- 4 tbsp. of sugar, granulated
- 1/4 tsp. of salt, kosher
- 1 1/2 tbsp. of vinegar, white
- 3 tomatoes, large
- 1/4 chopped onion, medium
- 1 tbsp. of oil, vegetable
- Pepper, ground

Instructions:

1. In medium-sized bowl, mix the water with salt and sugar. Use a spoon to stir till salt and sugar dissolve. Add the vinegar.

2. Dice the tomatoes and chop onion. Add to bowl.

3. Add and stir in oil. Add ground pepper. Refrigerate before you serve.

11 – Czech Stuffed Peppers

Czech grandmothers traditionally make pots of this dish in the winter months. The peppers are filling and satisfying.

Makes 8 Servings

Cooking + Prep Time: 3 hours 10 minutes

Ingredients:

- 8 large bell peppers, green
- 6 tbsp. of butter, unsalted
- 1 large, diced onion, yellow
- 1 1/2 lbs. of ground round
- 1 cup of uncooked rice, white
- Salt, kosher, as desired
- Pepper, ground, as desired
- 1 gallon of tomato juice, low sodium

Instructions:

1. Wash peppers well. Remove the stems and seeds. Rinse insides. Set the peppers aside.

2. In skillet on med., melt butter. Sauté onion till translucent.

3. In large bowl, combine butter mixture and onion with ground beef. Use your hands to combine. Season as desired. Add rice slowly. Mix well.

4. Stuff rice and meat mixture into peppers. Coat bottom of one or two pots with the oil. Place stuffed peppers in pots. Leave two inches at top of pot. Add tomato juice to cover peppers.

5. Heat mixture over low heat for two to three hours. Stir each 20-40 minutes as juice reduces to thicker sauce. When peppers look like their sides are splitting, they are done. Serve.

12 – Potato Soup

This could be called the queen of Czech soups. The traditional combination of potatoes, other veggies, mushrooms, herbs is filled with wonderful flavors.

Makes 4 Servings

Cooking + Prep Time: 45 minutes

Ingredients:

- 5 medium potatoes, diced
- 1/2 chopped onion
- 3 tbsp. of oil, olive or vegetable
- 3 large, diced carrots
- 2 tbsp. of garlic, minced
- 6 cloves
- 1 tsp. of salt, kosher
- 2 beef bouillon cubes
- 6 cups of water, filtered
- 2 diced stalks of celery
- 1 cup of sweet corn, white, frozen
- 1 tbsp. of marjoram, dry
- 1 cup of crushed and diced Portabella mushrooms, fresh
- Flour

Instructions:

1. In large pan, preheat oil. Sauté onion till translucent.

2. Add the minced garlic. Stir in corn, celery, potatoes and carrots. Stir while cooking for five or six minutes.

3. Add the water, beef bouillon, marjoram and salt. Bring to a boil. Add mushrooms. Allow to cook over med-high heat for 1/2 hour.

4. Mash larger pieces of potatoes.

5. Melt 4 tbsp. butter in frying pan. Add and stir 3 tbsp. flour. Combine well. It will be changing color while it is cooking. Remove from stove when it is light brown. Pour into boiling soup. Combine well. Allow to cook for five minutes longer. Serve.

13 – Bramboracky

These are traditional Czech potato pancakes, pan fried, and full of goodness. Many people eat them along with a beer.

Makes 3 Servings

Cooking + Prep Time: 55 minutes

Ingredients:

- 4 potatoes, large
- 3 crushed garlic cloves
- Salt, kosher, as desired
- Pepper, ground, as desired
- Optional: a pinch of marjoram, dried; 2 tsp. of caraway seeds
- 2 eggs, large
- 1 tbsp. of milk, whole
- 3 tbsp. of flour, all-purpose
- To fry: oil, vegetable

Instructions:

1. Peel, then grate potatoes coarsely. Squeeze out any liquid you can. Transfer grated potatoes to medium bowl. Add in garlic, kosher salt, marjoram, caraway seeds and pepper.

2. Beat eggs in milk. Add this mixture to potatoes. Combine well. Mix in flour gradually so your batter is thick, yet still pourable.

3. Heat 1/4 inch of oil in skillet on med-high. Spoon 1/4 of the batter into oil and flatten slightly. Fry pancakes till golden brown in color, three minutes per side or so. Drain on plate of paper towels. Repeat with remainder of batter and serve.

14 – Czech Mushroom Soup

Here is a classic soup made with mushrooms, cream, and dill. There are many versions of this recipe since almost every family has their own unique version. This is one of the best.

Makes 4 Servings

Cooking + Prep Time: 50 minutes

Ingredients:

- 6 potatoes, medium
- 1 container of sour cream
- 1 cup mushrooms
- 4 eggs, large
- 1 to 2 tbsp. vinegar, white
- 3 peppercorns
- 3 allspice
- Caraway
- 1 bay leaf, medium
- 2 tbsp. flour, all-purpose
- Butter, unsalted
- Dill
- Kosher salt

Instructions:

1. Clean, then slice mushrooms. Melt the butter in a pot. Stir-fry the mushrooms.

2. Add raw, cubed potatoes and spices. Season as desired. Add water to cover potatoes.

3. When the potatoes have softened, pull out spice. Add the flour and sour cream. Boil.

4. Season using chopped dill, vinegar and salt.

5. Break one egg. Place gently in boiled water with 1 spoon vinegar. Boil slowly for three to four minutes. Remove egg and place in cold, filtered water. Place egg into soup. Repeat with remaining eggs. Serve.

15 – Hot 'n Sour Soup

This soup bears little resemblance to the Asian version. It uses a spicy, vinegary broth with added shredded meat and tofu.

Makes 4 Servings

Cooking + Prep Time: 45 minutes

Ingredients:

- 4 cups of broth, chicken, low sodium
- 1/2 cup of diced mushrooms
- Optional: 1/4 cup of chicken, cooked and shredded
- 3 tbsp. of soy sauce, low sodium
- 1 tbsp. of garlic-chili paste
- 2 minced garlic cloves
- 3 oz. of drained, cubed tofu, firm
- Optional: 1/3 cup of matchstick-sliced bamboo shoots, canned
- 1/4 cup of vinegar, white
- 1/4 tsp. of white pepper, ground
- 2 tbsp. of water, cold
- 2 tbsp. of corn starch
- 1 egg, large
- 2 diced green onions
- 1 tsp. of sesame oil, toasted

Instructions:

1. Bring the broth to simmer in small pan. Add the chicken, mushrooms, chili paste, soy sauce and garlic cloves. Simmer for five minutes. Add the tofu, vinegar, white pepper and bamboo shoots. Simmer for five more minutes.

2. Combine water and the corn starch in cup. Stir till smooth, then add this to soup. Stir thoroughly. Allow to simmer till soup has thickened, five minutes or so longer.

3. Beat the egg in cup. Pour slowly into soup. Combine well. Heat for 1/2 minute. Add in sesame oil and green onions. Remove pan from heat and serve hot.

16 – Pasta Casserole

This dish, called Šunkofleky, is an inexpensive, easy, quick dinner. You can use any small pasta you prefer and your favorite meats or cheeses.

Makes 4 Servings

Cooking + Prep Time: 1 hour 5 minutes

Ingredients:

- 17 2/3 oz. of pasta
- 5 eggs, large
- 10 1/2 oz. of sausage, ham or other smoked meat
- Oil, vegetable
- Salt, kosher
- Pepper, ground

Instructions:

1. Preheat oven to 425F.

2. Boil the pasta using package instructions.

3. Cube the meat.

4. Mix meat and pasta together in an oven-safe pan.

5. Place in 425F oven for 12-15 minutes.

6. Whisk the eggs. Season as desired. Pour the eggs over meat and pasta. Lower oven temperature to 350F. Bake for 10-15 minutes more. Serve.

17 – Czech Garlic Soup

Garlic soup is frequently used at the start of meals in the Czech Republic. Like many recipes from this country, it usually includes chicken or beef broth and lots of butter or lard.

Makes 4 Servings

Cooking + Prep Time: 45 minutes

Ingredients:

- 2 tbsp. of butter, unsalted
- 1 chopped onion, small
- 1 tbsp. of caraway seeds
- 6 crushed garlic cloves
- 1 tsp. of salt, kosher +/- as desired
- 1/2 tsp. of pepper, ground
- 5 cups of water, filtered
- 1 tbsp. of chicken bouillon
- 3 diced potatoes
- Croutons, prepared

Instructions:

1. Heat butter in medium pot on med. heat. Add garlic and onion. Cook till onion is translucent and soft, three to five minutes.

2. Add kosher salt, caraway seeds and ground pepper. Cook for a minute more. Add the water. Mix in the bouillon. Bring the soup to boil, five minutes or so. Add the diced potatoes. Make sure the water covers the potatoes by several inches.

3. Reduce the heat level to simmer. Cook till potatoes become soft, 15-20 minutes. Don't allow them to get mushy. Serve with the prepared croutons.

18 – Fried Carp

Fried carp has always been a traditional recipe for Christmas Eve. If carp is not available in your area, you can use cod, pollock, or haddock.

Makes 2-4 Servings

Cooking + Prep Time: 35 minutes + 1 hour sitting time

Ingredients:

- 3 lbs. of carp
- Flour, all-purpose
- 1 egg, large, beaten
- Salt, kosher
- To fry: butter, unsalted
- Breadcrumbs
- Lemon, fresh
- Parsley fresh

Instructions:

1. Clean one carp. Divide it into portions.

2. Wash the fish, then sprinkle with kosher salt. Set for one hour.

3. Dry fish with cloth. Dip it in flour, then beaten egg and breadcrumbs. Quickly fry in the hot butter.

4. When fish has turned golden-brown in color on both sides, lower heat. Allow to gently cook till done.

5. Garnish using parsley and lemon. Serve.

19 – Goose Giblets

Here is another dish that is often served during the Christmas holidays. It is frequently made to accompany roasted Christmas goose.

Makes 4 Servings

Cooking + Prep Time: 55 minutes

Ingredients:

- 8 tbsp. of fat
- 2 chopped onions, small
- 1 1/2 cups of giblets, goose or turkey
- 2 tsp. of paprika, sweet
- 1 tsp. of caraway seeds
- Kosher salt, as desired
- 3/4 cup of stock, beef
- 7 tbsp. of sour cream, low fat
- 7 tbsp. of cream, heavy

Instructions:

1. Heat the fat in large pan on med. heat. Stir and cook onions in fat till they are tender, five minutes or so.

2. Sprinkle the giblets with caraway, salt and paprika. Add to pan. Fry till giblets have browned, five to seven minutes.

3. Add stock. Reduce the heat level to low. Simmer till the giblets soften, 20 minutes or so. Add heavy cream and sour cream. Simmer till heated fully through, five more minutes. Serve.

20 – Paprika Green Beans

These spiced green beans are a quick, simple side dish to serve with the protein of your main dish. They are flavored with smoked paprika for a traditional Czech taste.

Makes 4 Servings

Cooking + Prep Time: 1 hour 20 minutes

Ingredients:

- 2 quarts of water, filtered
- 1 tsp. of salt, kosher
- 1 lb. of green beans, sliced in 1" pieces
- 4 tbsp. of butter, unsalted
- 3/4 cup of onions, chopped finely
- 1 tbsp. of paprika, sweet
- 2 tbsp. of flour, all-purpose
- 1 cup of sour cream, light
- 1/2 tsp. of salt, kosher

Instructions:

1. In medium saucepan, bring 2 quarts water + tsp. salt to boil on high heat. Then drop beans in by handfuls.

2. Bring water back to boil. Lower heat to med. Cook beans for 12-15 minutes, till barely tender. Immediately drain beans.

3. Melt butter in heavy skillet. When it stops foaming, add onions. Cook for four to five minutes, till onions become translucent. Off heat, stir in paprika and continue to stir till onions are coated well.

4. Beat flour into sour cream with whisk. Stir mixture in skillet with onions. Salt as desired. Simmer over low heat for four to five minutes, till sauce is creamy and smooth. Stir in beans gently. Simmer for five more minutes, till heated fully through. Serve.

21 – Roasted Beef Goulash

Beef goulash is one of the most often-made dinner recipes in the Czech Republic. You can serve it with potato or bread dumplings, rice, pasta, or Czech bread.

Makes 6 Servings

Cooking + Prep Time: 45 minutes

Ingredients:

- 3 pounds of rump roast, beef
- 3 onions, diced
- 12 tbsp. of oil, vegetable
- 1 1/2 tbsp. of garlic, minced
- 2 tsp. of marjoram
- 3 tsp. of salt, kosher
- 3 tsp. of paprika, Hungarian sweet
- 1 beef bouillon cube

Instructions:

1. Dice the onion. Sauté with the oil in pressure cooker with no lid on, till a golden brown in color.

2. Cut the meat into small-sized cubes. Add to onions. Cover pressure cooker with lid. Don't lock the lid yet.

3. Meat will release some water. Remove lid and add marjoram, paprika, bouillon, garlic and kosher salt. Place lid back on. Cook till all liquid has absorbed or evaporated.

4. Add a cup of filtered water. Cook till it is again gone, and meat begins sticking to bottom of pot.

5. Pour in 4 additional cups of filtered water. Close lid tightly. Bring to a boil, then turn temperature down to med-low. Cook for 18-20 minutes.

6. Check meat for tenderness. Place pot in sink. Run cold tap water over top so the lid unlocks.

7. Mix a cup of filtered water with 1/4 cup flour in medium bowl, thoroughly. Pour into sauce. Cook for three to five minutes more.

8. Chop 1/2 onion. Stir into sauce. Serve with dumplings, pasta or rice.

22 – Fried Veal

There are many variations of this recipe, but it is traditionally made with veal fillets and ham. You could also use pork or beef and extra chopped onions.

Makes 4 Servings

Cooking + Prep Time: 35 minutes

Ingredients:

- 4 veal fillet slices
- 2 ounces of chopped ham
- Salt, kosher
- 1 tbsp. of flour, all-purpose
- 1 egg, large
- 1 tbsp. of milk, 2%
- 1 ounce of butter, unsalted
- 1 tsp. of breadcrumbs, fine
- To fry: 4 ounces of fat
- Green peas

Instructions:

1. Trim meat. Beat it lightly, then season with kosher salt.

2. Scramble egg in pan along with butter, ham and peas.

3. Spread a bit of this mixture on all veal pieces. Fold them in halves. Secure with skewers.

4. Dip meat carefully in flour, then milk, then breadcrumbs. Fry in heated fat and serve.

23 -- Fried Potato Balls

In Czech restaurants, you'll often find these served as side dishes. This is an easy recipe that allows you to bring the taste into your home.

Makes 5 Servings

Cooking + Prep Time: 45 minutes

Ingredients:

- 4 cups of peeled, diced potatoes
- 1 tsp. of salt, kosher
- 3 cups of water, filtered
- 3 egg, medium
- 1/4 cup of hot cereal, Farina® or similar
- 1 cup of flour, all-purpose
- 1 tsp. of salt, kosher
- 2 tbsp. of milk, low fat
- Breadcrumbs
- Oil, cooking

Instructions:

1. Peel, then dice the potatoes. Cook for 20-25 minutes in three cups filtered water and 1 tsp. kosher salt.

2. Drain water off. Mash potatoes till lump-free. Allow to cool.

3. Place potatoes on flat work surface. Add the egg, hot cereal, salt and flour. Knead by hand into a smooth dough.

4. Form quarter-sized balls from dough.

5. In small-sized bowl, beat two eggs in 2 tbsp. milk with 1/2 tsp. salt added.

6. Taking four balls of potato at one time, coat in egg mixture. Spoon balls out with slotted spoon, allowing excess egg to drip back in bowl.

7. Prepare a separate bowl with the breadcrumbs. Coat balls in crumbs. Place on plate.

8. Preheat 1/2-inch of oil in frying pan. Place balls in batches in pan. Reduce temperature to med. Cook till balls are golden brown in color. Be sure to cook all sides.

9. Remove balls from the pan. Place in paper-towel-lined bowl. Sprinkle with a bit more salt. Serve.

24 – Sauerkraut Potato Salad

This is a hearty salad that plays the potatoes and sauerkraut well against each other. It is usually served during the winter months, with main dishes of veal or pork.

Makes 4-6 Servings

Cooking + Prep Time: 45 minutes

Ingredients:

- 4 washed potatoes, medium
- Salt, kosher
- 3 cups of sauerkraut, drained
- 1 peeled, chopped onion, medium
- 1/4 cup of oil, salad
- 2 tbsp. of vinegar, cider
- 2 tsp. of sugar, granulated
- 1/2 tsp. of caraway seeds
- Pepper, ground, as desired
- 1 scraped, grated carrot, large

Instructions:

1. Cook the potatoes in skins in a bit of lightly salted, boiling filtered water till they are tender, 20-25 minutes.

2. Peel the potatoes and slice while they are still warm.

3. Next, combine potatoes with onions and sauerkraut in large sized bowl.

4. Mix oil, vinegar, sugar, caraway seeds, kosher salt ground pepper together.

5. Add mixture from step 4 to the vegetable mixture. Combine well.

6. Sprinkled with the grated carrots and serve.

25 – Cucumber Salad

This cucumber salad with vinegar is refreshing and delicious and totally easy to make at home. It is often served in Czech homes, restaurants, and even school cafeterias.

Makes 3-4 Servings

Cooking + Prep Time: 25 minutes

Ingredients:

- 1 cucumber, salad
- 1/2 cup of water, filtered
- 6 tbsp. of sugar, granulated
- 1/4 tsp. of salt, kosher
- 3 tbsp. of vinegar, white
- Pepper, ground

Instructions:

1. Peel cucumbers. Grind with cheese grater in bowl, using large holes to make very thin slices.

2. Add and stir in kosher salt and mix. Allow to rest for five minutes or so. Cucumber will release its juices.

3. Add the sugar. Mix till it has dissolved. Add vinegar, water and ground pepper.

4. Mix thoroughly. Cover. Place in the refrigerator and allow to chill. Serve.

Czech desserts are made in various ways, but they are all delicious. Make one of these soon...

26 – Czech Babovka – Marble Cake

This marble cake is a sweet treat that is typically found in Czech bakeries. Czech families fondly remember marble cakes on the table at Grandmother's house.

Makes 8 Servings

Cooking + Prep Time: 1 hour 55 minutes

Ingredients:

- 11 2/3 ounces of flour, soft wheat
- 11 2/3 ounces of sugar, icing
- 4 1/4 fluid ounces of milk, 2%
- 6 1/3 oz. butter, unsalted, softened
- 4 eggs, large
- 1 tsp. baking soda
- 1 tsp. cocoa, unsweetened

Instructions:

1. Preheat oven to 350F.

2. Place butter, egg yolks and sugar in bowl of food processor. Mix well.

3. Mix baking soda with sugar and flour. Add this mixture slowly into mixture from step 2. Combine well.

4. Whip the egg whites. Add to dough.

5. Separate 1/3 dough. Add cocoa to that part and mix.

6. Grease marble cake form with butter. Sprinkle with soft wheat flour.

7. Place one light part of dough in form. Follow with dark (cocoa) dough and then the last 1/3 of light dough.

8. Place pan in 350F oven and bake for 45-50 minutes.

9. Remove pan from oven. Allow to set for five minutes or so. Remove from pan. Sprinkle with icing sugar and serve.

27 – Czech Bublanina

These Czech cakes vary with the fruits of the seasons. The texture may remind you of coffee cake and commonly includes blueberries, strawberries, apricots, nectarines, plums, or cherries.

Makes 6 Servings

Cooking + Prep Time: 1 hour 10 minutes

Ingredients:

- 1/2 cup of butter, softened
- 1/2 cup of sugar, granulated
- 3 room temperature eggs, large
- Optional: 1 tbsp. liqueur, orange
- 1 tsp. of zest, orange
- 1/2 tsp. of salt, kosher
- 1 cup of flour, all-purpose
- A pinch cream of tartar
- 2 cups of washed, stemmed blueberries, fresh
- For garnishing: sugar, powdered
- Optional: sauce, blueberry

Instructions:

1. Place a rack in middle of the oven. Heat oven to 350F. Butter 9" square baking pan.

2. In medium sized bowl, cream butter, yolks and sugar together till fluffy and light. Add the orange liqueur, if desired. Add orange zest and kosher salt and mix well.

3. In separate medium sized bowl, beat the egg whites with the cream of tartar till stiff. Fold this into the butter and egg yolk mixture.

4. Add the batter to pan prepared above. Scatter fresh blueberries over the top evenly. Press them down a bit into batter using a spatula. Bake for 35-40 minutes, till toothpick pushed into cake near the middle comes back clean. Dust with powdered sugar. Add blueberry sauce if you like. Slice and serve.

28 – Grandmother's Houska

This sweet bread is typically made during the Christmas holidays. It is prepared for Christmas Day, but you may not be able to resist sneaking a few pieces on Christmas Eve.

Makes 10 Servings

Cooking + Prep Time: 1 hour + 2 1/2-hours standing time

Ingredients:

- 1 cup of milk, low fat
- 3/4 cup of sugar, granulated
- 10 tbsp. of butter + extra for brushing, as desired
- 1 tsp. of salt, kosher
- 2 x 1/4-oz. envelopes of dry yeast, active
- 1 whole egg, large
- 3 yolks from large eggs
- 5-6 cups of flour, all-purpose
- 1/4 tsp. of mace, ground
- 1/2 cup of raisins, golden, + extra as desired

Instructions:

1. Combine the milk sugar in small pan on high heat. Then heat till small bubbles start appearing around the edges of pan. Remove pan from heat and stir in the butter till it melts. Add the salt. Allow the mixture to cool off a bit. It should still be somewhat warm, though.

2. Dissolve the active yeast in 1/4 cup of warm, filtered water. Transfer the milk mixture to stand mixer with paddle attachment fitted. Add the yeast mixture. Beat in a whole egg plus the 3 yolks.

3. Add mace and 3 cups of flour. Beat till smooth. Fit your mixer with a dough hook. Add remainder of flour, 1/2 cup after another, and mix thoroughly after each 1/2 cup. Dough should be elastic and smooth, and not sticky. Add the raisins and combine well.

4. Sprinkle a bit of flour over the dough. Place dough in large sized bowl. Cover it with a towel. Allow to rise in warm area of your house for an hour and a half, till its bulk doubles.

5. Place the dough on floured work surface. Divide it into eight balls. Three balls should be large – the size of softballs. Three should be medium – the size of tennis balls. Two should be smaller – a bit larger in size than golf balls.

6. Knead balls well. Roll the larger balls into 16" ropes. Braid them together. Place on baking pan. Repeat this step with the medium balls. Place that braid atop first one. Repeat steps with smaller balls and place that braid atop second one. Cover dough. Allow to rise for an hour.

7. Heat oven to 325F. Brush the bread using melted butter, if you like. Bake in 325F oven for 30-40 minutes. Serve warm.

29 – Ice Cream Kolacky

The dough in this kolacky recipe is richer because it has ice cream added. Using canned filling means it's easier and quicker to make.

Makes 12 Servings

Cooking + Prep Time: 1 hour 5 minutes + 8 hours refrigeration time

Ingredients:

- 1 pint of ice cream, vanilla
- 2 cups of butter, unsalted
- 4 cups of flour, all-purpose
- 1/2 cup of any flavor fruit preserves

Instructions:

1. Add the flour to unsalted butter. Crumble them in a pastry blender. Add the ice cream. Attach dough hooks and work mixture into dough. When it is smooth, shape dough into a ball. Place in refrigerator overnight.

2. Next day, preheat the oven to 350F.

3. Roll dough on floured work surface to 1/8" thickness. Use rim of glass to cut out circles in dough. Place on baking sheet, and make indentation in middle of circles. Fill those indentations with 1/2 tsp. of fruit filling.

4. Bake in 350F oven for 18-20 minutes. Use powdered sugar to sprinkle them when they have cooled. Serve.

30 – Listy Cookies

These cookies, pronounced LISS-tay, are a recipe from a Czech grandmother. It just doesn't get any more genuine than that.

Makes 18 Servings

Cooking + Prep Time: 55 minutes

Ingredients:

- 1 cup of sugar, granulated
- 1 cup of cream
- 4 eggs, large
- 1/4 tsp. of salt, kosher
- Flour, to help in making dough stiff

Instructions:

1. Mix all the ingredients. Roll out on a pre-floured work surface like you would if making noodles.

2. Cut into 3" wide strips with pizza cutter. Cut again in small sized diamonds.

3. Fry the diamonds in 375F grease.

4. Turn once, frying till they are a light golden in color.

5. Remove diamonds from grease. Drain on plate lined with paper towels.

6. Sprinkle with powdered sugar and serve.

Conclusion

This Czech cookbook has shown you…

How to use different ingredients to affect unique Bohemian tastes in dishes both well-known and rare.

How can you include Czech recipes in your home cooking?

You can…

- Make beef goulash, which I imagine everyone knows about. It is just as tasty as you have heard.

- Learn to cook with sweet paprika, which is widely used in the Czech Republic. Find it in the spice aisle of your local market.

- Enjoy making the delectable seafood dishes of Europe, including carp and trout. Fish is not a mainstay in the Czech Republic, but there are SO many ways to make it great.

- Make dishes using potatoes and dumplings, which are often used in Czech cooking.

- Make various types of desserts like Bábovka and Listy cookies, which will tempt your family's sweet tooth.

Have fun experimenting! Enjoy the results!

About the Author

Allie Allen developed her passion for the culinary arts at the tender age of five when she would help her mother cook for their large family of 8. Even back then, her family knew this would be more than a hobby for the young Allie and when she graduated from high school, she applied to cooking school in London. It had always been a dream of the young chef to study with some of Europe's best and she made it happen by attending the Chef Academy of London.

After graduation, Allie decided to bring her skills back to North America and open up her own restaurant. After 10 successful years as head chef and owner, she decided to sell her business and pursue other career avenues. This monumental decision led Allie to her true calling, teaching. She also started to write e-books for her students to study at home for practice. She is now the proud author of several e-books and gives private and semi-private cooking lessons to a range of students at all levels of experience.

Stay tuned for more from this dynamic chef and teacher when she releases more informative e-books on cooking and baking in the near future. Her work is infused with stores and anecdotes you will love!

Author's Afterthoughts

I can't tell you how grateful I am that you decided to read my book. My most heartfelt thanks that you took time out of your life to choose my work and I hope you find benefit within these pages.

There are so many books available today that offer similar content so that makes it even more humbling that you decided to buying mine.

Tell me what you thought! I am eager to hear your opinion and ideas on what you read as are others who are looking for a good book to buy. Leave a review on Amazon.com so others can benefit from your wisdom!

With much thanks,

Allie Allen

Printed in Great Britain
by Amazon

35298902R00051